Animals of Africa

GORILLAS

by Tammy Gagne

FOCUS READERS

FOCUS READERS

www.focusreaders.com

Focus Readers is distributed by North Star Editions:
sales@northstareditions.com | 888-417-0195

Produced for Focus Readers by Red Line Editorial.

Photographs ©: guenterguni/iStockphoto, cover, 1; Goddard_Photography/iStockphoto, 4–5; LMspencer/Shutterstock Images, 7; Gudkov Andrey/Shutterstock Images, 8, 20–21; Emi/Shutterstock Images, 10–11, 13; Erik Zandboer/Shutterstock Images, 15; Sergey Uryadnikov/Shutterstock Images, 16–17; Eric Isselee/Shutterstock Images, 19; Rpictures/iStockphoto, 22 (top); Mary Ann McDonald/Shutterstock Images, 22 (bottom left); Rob Hainer/Shutterstock Images, 22 (bottom right); bimserd/Shutterstock Images, 24, 29; Bettmann/Getty Images, 27

ISBN
978-1-63517-264-5 (hardcover)
978-1-63517-329-1 (paperback)
978-1-63517-459-5 (ebook pdf)
978-1-63517-394-9 (hosted ebook)

Library of Congress Control Number: 2017935137

Printed in the United States of America
Mankato, MN
June, 2017

About the Author

Tammy Gagne has written more than 150 books for adults and children. She resides in northern New England with her husband and son. One of her favorite pastimes is visiting schools to talk to kids about the writing process.

TABLE OF CONTENTS

CHAPTER 1

WORK, REST, REPEAT

The mountain gorillas have had a busy day. They spent the morning **foraging**. They are ready to rest. Adult gorillas need a chance to interact. They communicate and relax while young gorillas play.

Young mountain gorillas climb in the trees.

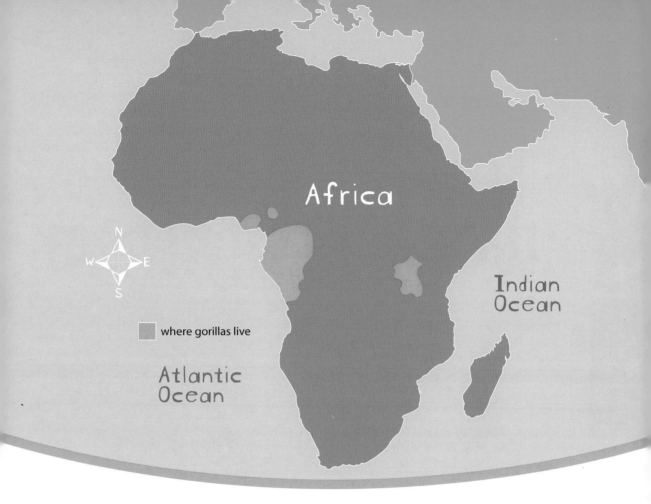

Africa

Indian
Ocean

where gorillas live

Atlantic
Ocean

 Gorilla can be found in only a few areas of Africa.

Gorillas live in Africa. They can
have different **habitats**. Some live
on the slopes of large mountains.
They might even live on volcanoes.

 A young gorilla hangs from a branch.

Others can be found in forests.
Gorillas can climb trees. But most
stay on the ground.

 A mountain gorilla walks through the forest.

Four types of gorillas live in Africa. Eastern lowland gorillas live in central Africa. Mountain gorillas live in central Africa, too. They live in the Virunga Mountains. Two types of gorillas live in western Africa. These are western lowland gorillas and cross river gorillas.

FUN FACT

A gorilla's territory can be as large as 16 square miles (41 sq. km).

CHAPTER 2

BIG AND HAIRY

Gorillas have dark skin. Their bodies are hairy. The hair color depends on the type of gorilla. Many gorillas are black. But their hair can be brown or gray, too.

Western lowland gorillas have dark hair covering their bodies.

Gorillas are the largest of all **primates** on Earth. Males weigh approximately 375 pounds (170 kg). Females are lighter than males. They weigh approximately 200 pounds (91 kg).

Adult male gorillas are approximately 5.5 feet (1.7 m) tall.

 Gorillas often walk on all four limbs.

Females are a little shorter. They are approximately 4.8 feet (1.5 m) tall as adults.

Eastern lowland gorillas are the largest type of gorilla. The western lowland gorilla is the smallest.

A gorilla's arms are longer than its legs. Having such long arms makes it easy for the animal to walk on all four limbs. Because of this, gorillas are called **quadrupeds**.

FUN FACT

When gorillas walk on all four limbs, it is called knuckle walking.

 A large male gorilla stands in a tree.

CHAPTER 3

SURVIVAL TRAITS

Gorillas have many traits that help them survive in the wild. Their arm muscles are larger than those in their legs. This arm strength helps gorillas when foraging. They can bend and break large plants.

A gorilla breaks a branch to eat.

An adult male gorilla is six times stronger than an adult man.

Gorillas have **opposable** thumbs. This helps a gorilla grab objects and move them. Gorillas also have an opposable toe on each foot. These toes allow gorillas to use their feet like hands.

Mountain gorillas live in cold areas. The air in the mountains can drop below freezing. But these

PARTS OF A GORILLA

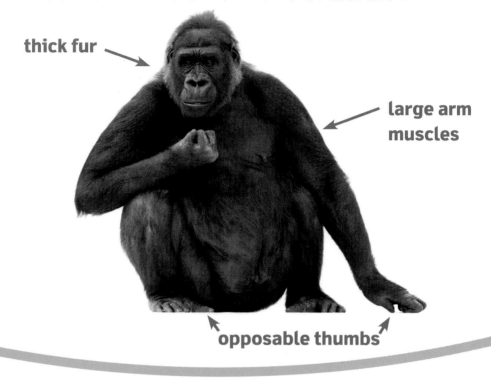

thick fur

large arm muscles

opposable thumbs

gorillas have long, thick fur. When the weather gets cold, the gorillas huddle together. They stay close together for long periods. The gorillas use each other's body heat to stay warm.

CHAPTER 4

GORILLA BEHAVIOR

Gorillas live in groups called troops. Troops include several adult gorillas. Female gorillas have one baby at a time. Babies are called infants. They stay close to their mothers for up to three years.

 A female gorilla holds her baby.

GORILLA LIFE CYCLE

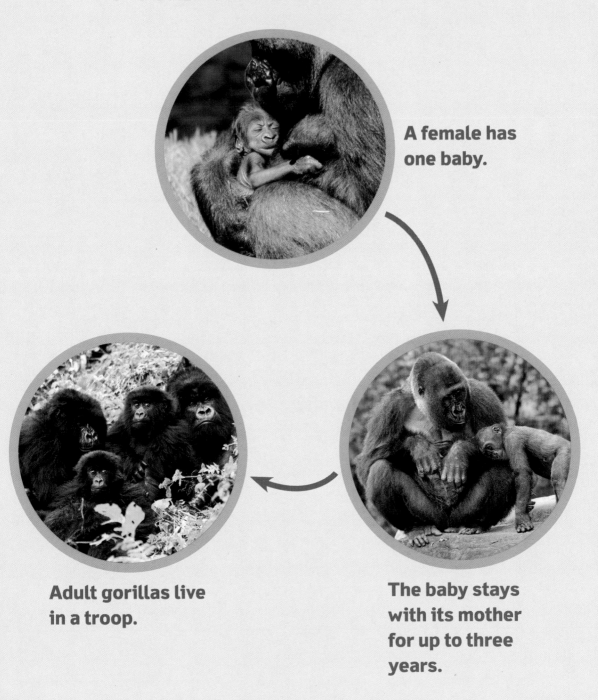

A female has one baby.

The baby stays with its mother for up to three years.

Adult gorillas live in a troop.

Usually, the oldest male leads the troop. He decides all of the troop's activities. For example, he chooses when the troop wakes up, eats, and sleeps each day. This leader often pounds his chest with his hands.

If another animal threatens the troop, the leader might charge at it. He defends his family.

FUN FACT

Gorillas usually live between 30 and 50 years.

 Adult males have silver hair on their backs.

Adult male gorillas are called silverbacks. This name comes from the silver hair on their backs. Younger males are called blackbacks.

Most gorillas are **herbivores**. Gorillas often eat leaves and roots. Their large, strong teeth help them chew twigs and tree bark. They also eat fruits. Some gorillas might eat insects, too. They use their **molars** to grind hard substances.

KOKO

Gorillas are intelligent animals. One of the smartest gorillas in the world lives at a research facility in California. Her name is Koko. Researcher Francine Patterson began teaching Koko sign language in 1972. At that time, Koko was just one year old. Today she knows more than 1,000 words. Experts compare her vocabulary with that of a human three-year-old.

Koko has even invented signs for words Patterson did not teach her. After seeing barrettes in people's hair, Koko raised her hand to her head. She then moved her hand forward. She was showing Patterson where a barrette is placed. Koko kept making this

Koko uses the sign for listen.

sign until the researcher figured out what
the gorilla meant.

FOCUS ON
GORILLAS

Write your answers on a separate piece of paper.

1. Write a sentence explaining the main idea of Chapter 3.

2. What do you think is a gorilla's most interesting trait? Explain your answer.

3. Which gorilla decides when it is time for the group to eat?
    A. the oldest male
    B. the oldest female
    C. the youngest male

4. Why might gorillas move faster walking on all four limbs than on their hind legs?
    A. because the muscles in their legs are stronger
    B. because the muscles in their thumbs are weak
    C. because the muscles in their arms are stronger

5. What does **interact** mean in this book?

Adult gorillas need a chance to interact. They communicate and relax while young gorillas play.

    A. find food and eat
    B. communicate and connect
    C. rest and relax

6. What does **huddle** mean in this book?

When the weather gets cold, the gorillas huddle together. They stay close together for long periods.

    A. get close together
    B. separate
    C. run away

Answer key on page 32.

GLOSSARY

foraging
Searching for food.

habitats
The type of places where plants or animals normally grow or live.

herbivores
Animals that eat mostly plants.

molars
The flat teeth used for grinding food.

opposable
Capable of being placed against another finger or toe.

primates
Mammals with hands that can grasp things.

quadrupeds
Animals that walk on four limbs.

TO LEARN MORE

BOOKS

Hirsch, Rebecca E. *Mountain Gorillas: Powerful Forest Mammals*. Minneapolis: Lerner Publications, 2015.

Stevens, Kathryn. *Gorillas*. North Mankato, MN: The Child's World, 2015.

Wang, Andrea. *Gorillas*. Edina, MN: Abdo Publishing, 2014.

NOTE TO EDUCATORS

Visit **www.focusreaders.com** to find lesson plans, activities, links, and other resources related to this title.

INDEX

Answer Key: 1. Answers will vary; **2.** Answers will vary; **3.** A; **4.** C; **5.** B; **6.** A